Beyond Hello

Beyond Hello

How to spot the hidden
messages in everyday
conversation

Norman Markel, Ph.D.
Trisha Renaud

Table of Contents

Introduction

On any given day, each of us is likely to engage in dozens of conversations, some hurried and casual, others lengthy and intense.

We toss quick greetings to neighbors or friends we encounter. We trade ideas with co-workers when we meet to assess a project or evaluate performance goals. We may have lunch and share laughs with a friend, or have more serious dialogue at a doctor's appointment. We may linger for conversation with a dinner date or wind up the day with give-and-take around the family dinner table.

And along the way, we encounter store clerks, bank tellers, fellow health enthusiasts at the gym, and any number of others.

In short, conversation, whether brief or long, inconsequential or substantive, is a central part of our social life.

Countless lectures and how-to books have been

written on the topic of the "art" of conversation. They provide us with tactics for initiating conversation, advice on which subjects to discuss and which to avoid, rules for the polite way to address strangers, and guidance on how to conduct an interview or be interviewed.

Conversation is also the subject of scholarly scrutiny. Linguists in the field of conversation analysis, known as CA, take apart entire dialogues. They look for the order, sequence and patterns of the conversation, including turn-taking and interruptions.

Most of us, however, rarely turn an analytic eye on our own conversations. We have little time or incentive to look back at what was said, how it was said or our behavior during any particular conversation. This failure, however, means that we miss important information about those with whom we speak, as well as about ourselves.

Is the boss really as much of a friend as he or she says? Is your love interest signaling that you're an equal partner or that he or she has the upper hand in the relationship? Even more important, how do you come across – as an equal or someone superior?

The answers to those questions are simpler than you might think.

No matter what the topic of discussion, all of us display certain behaviors when we converse that are indicative of how we feel about each other. Seemingly inconsequential behaviors that we exhibit when we speak to one another can reveal much about the politics at the core of our relationships.

The behavioral signs of power, status and friendship – sometimes referred to as hierarchy and solidarity–these are the micropolitics of conversation.

The prefix "micro" in the word micropolitics might mean small but it does *not* mean insignificant.

Micropolitics concerns the ways in which power operates to influence our everyday actions and relationships. It plays out in conflict and competition, as well as cooperation and support.

In other words, it is politics brought to bear on the most routine and intimate of our daily interactions. Or, as 1970's women's movement activists stressed, "The personal is political."

Our everyday interactions – smiles, gestures, distances and words – not only reflect the political and social structure of our society, but defend and maintain it. Those who want to build relationships based on friendship rather than power, solidarity rather than hierarchy or status, would do well to cultivate an awareness of the messages displayed in even the most mundane of conversations.

Chapter One

The Clues in Conversation

People who are engaged in conversation invariably display clues about their attitudes and what is going on in their relationship. A casual observer can spot some of these signals, even at a distance.

Try a little "conversation watching" the next time you are at a restaurant and see what you can learn. For example, you might see a couple cuddled together in a booth, side by side, holding hands and gazing into each other's eyes. They are clearly in love.

Another couple may be seated opposite each other. This time, the man seems to be doing most of the talking, punctuating his words with his fork while the woman mostly stares at her plate. It's clearly not a very close relationship. The woman is either bored or intimidated by her dinner companion.

Chapter 1— The Clues in Conversation

Watching individuals who are engaged in conversation from a distance may not allow you to guess every detail about the relationships you see, but you can get a sense of the attitudes at work. You could no doubt discover more if you could overhear the conversation.

The clues to the politics of a conversation are easily spotted, *if* you know what the clues are and what they mean. The behavioral clues express either hierarchy or solidarity, that is, a status relationship or a friendship relationship.

The dimensions of hierarchy and solidarity are not black and white; rather, they exist on a continuum. People can be of lesser, greater or equal rank. They can be close friends, casual acquaintances or strangers. One can be of a greater rank (hierarchy), yet interact with another as an equal (solidarity).

So what are these clues?

The most important are these:

Address: what we call a person in greeting

Self-disclosure: the amount of personal information and feelings we discuss

Seating: how we position ourselves in relation to the other person

Eye contact: how much we look at each other

Touch: the degree/extent of physical contact

In the example at the beginning of this chapter, the couples were displaying three of the vital signs of conversation – *touch, seating arrangement and eye contact.* The first couple sat side by side, holding hands, both indicators of closeness. The second couple sat on opposite sides of the table. Perhaps most telling of all, the woman could not bring herself to maintain eye contact and the man, oblivious to her discomfort, prattled on. He was clearly in charge of the conversation whether she liked it or not.

Those three nonverbal signs, along with the two verbal signs *address and self-disclosure,* are the stealth dimensions of conversation. That is, they provide critical clues to how we feel about each other, to the micropolitics of that conversation and that relationship.

In any given conversation, whether consciously or not, we communicate our attitudes toward the other person. We signal how friendly we are – the solidarity element – as well as our perceived social status – the hierarchy element. We are seldom, however, aware of the message our conversational behaviors send. As a result, we often send unintentional signals to others that may hurt our relationships with friends, co-workers, neighbors or loved ones. While a parent may speak to a child in a top-down way, they may also exhibit the same behavior in speaking to a spouse, with unintended consequences. A supervisor who exhibits signs of hierarchy rather than solidarity to employees may have difficulty encouraging them to be candid about problems on the job.

In addition, the more differences that exist between two people, such as class, race/ethnicity, gender or sexual orientation, the more likely they are to misinterpret the meaning of another's behavior.

But if one pays attention to the clues of conversation and to the context in which they occur, such misinterpretations can be avoided.

Fortunately, each of us can become aware of and control these five vital signs – address, seating arrangement, self-disclosure, eye contact and touch.

Why only five vital signs? Obviously, we display other behaviors during conversation that can be important in communication, such as interruptions, gesturing and turn-taking.

The five signs named above, however, have certain characteristics that make them the most important.

They are *universal.* That is, they are common to all cultures and all settings.

They are *easily identifiable* by the average person without special tools or training.

Finally, they are *based on science.* Social scientists have studied them over the years, and, while social mores may change, these behaviors remain the most indicative clues to our attitudes and outlooks.

The following chapters will examine each vital sign, its manifestations and meaning, as well as the scientific research on it.

This book includes responses from an internet survey in which respondents described their experiences with each of the five vital signs of conversation. The sample responses cited are from a selected group of seven survey participants, chosen for diversity of age, gender and ethnicity.

One caveat: Since the signs of seating, touch and eye contact are nonverbal behaviors, they are obviously only present when the parties are face-to-face. That means there are fewer clues present in the multitude of email and text messages we send on a daily basis. This may be why emoticons are so popular in electronic messages. They help us express the emotions behind the words and ensure the receiver gets the message.

Chapter Two
Terms of Endearment,
Terms of Estrangement

A term or form of address, quite simply, is what we call someone when we greet them.

The greeting we choose might be on the formal side, such as a title combined with that person's last name (Mr. Presley). Then again, it could be semi-formal or just downright casual, such as "Elvis" or a nickname like "Dude."

In any event, our choice of how to address someone sends a message about how we regard them. Do we see them as a friend, an equal or as someone distant, of lower or higher status? Terms of address clarify the relationship between two people in a way we intuitively, but not always consciously, understand.

In general, a domineering or autocratic attitude (*hierarchy*) is conveyed by an unequal exchange of terms between two people, while an intimate and friendly one (*solidarity*) involves an exchange of equal terms.

Many languages, although not English, utilize forms of pronouns to distinguish a formal or status relationship from a casual or friendly one. For example, in French, the pronoun "you" changes depending on the situation. Speakers use *vous* for a stranger or someone of higher status but switch to "tu" when addressing a friend.[1]

In English, however, the pronouns remain the same, regardless of the relationship. Instead, the terms of address change. Those may include:

First names such as Robert

Nicknames such as "Bobby"

Last names such as Williams

Titles/Honorifics such as Mr., Ms., Sir, Ma'am or Doctor

The basics

Researchers first systematically examined how we use forms of address in 1961.[2] That's when Roger Brown and Marguerite Ford combined a survey of the greetings used in scripts of American plays and various recorded conversations, along with their observations of how employees of a Boston business interacted. Several years later, other researchers conducted an in-depth look at interpersonal communication at an insurance firm,[3] interviewing 87 employees at four different organizational levels. Both studies examined terms of address as they relate to status relations (hierarchy) and to intimate or friendly (solidarity) relations. They concluded that:

• If the individuals are of the same status, the greetings they offer one another are reciprocal and are typically of the friendlier form, such as a first name or nickname.

• However, when two people differ in status (such as a supervisor and subordinate), the terms of address they use are not reciprocal. The individual of a higher status is referred to by his/her title and last name, while the person of lower status is greeted with a more casual and friendly form such as a first name or nickname.

• The address form used between intimates (first name or nickname) is also used by higher status individuals to address so-called inferiors.

• The person who holds the higher status will typically be the one who initiates movement toward more intimate, friendlier relations and more egalitarian forms of address.

Let's look at what these findings might mean in an everyday encounter. When two good friends hail each other, they most often use first names as a greeting.

"Barbara! How are you?"

"I'm great, Janice. And it's great to see you."

But if the two people who encounter one another are merely casual acquaintances, they are more likely to use a title, plus a last name.

"It's been a long time since I've seen you out in the neighborhood, Mr. McDonald. How have you been?"

"I've been busy with work, Mrs. Jones, and just haven't had the chance for my walks."

However, when the two people greeting each other are of unequal status, the forms of address are not reciprocal.

"It seems you're late for work today, Walter."

"I know Mr. Sammons and I'm sorry. Traffic was really bad."

First naming

In the example above, the supervisor, being of a higher status, uses employee Walter's first name but is accorded a title and last name when he is addressed. The use of first names to designate lower status does not only occur in this context. For years in the South, whites called blacks by their first names or by the term "boy" or "girl" irrespective of how well-acquainted they were. On the other hand, blacks were expected to address whites using a higher-status term such as Mr. Miller or Miss Mary.

While such racist practices have ceased to be widespread, a 1984 study found that blacks tended to distrust whites who addressed them by first names in the workplace and preferred the use of formal terms of address. The study also found that whites in the same situation more frequently preferred informal address.[4]

Clearly, calling someone one doesn't know well by his or her first name can be a method of establishing control of the relationship on the spot. That's why police frequently call suspects by the first name, particularly during interrogations. But it may well be an attempt to establish a friendly relationship on the spot, as when politicians being interviewed call reporters by their first name.

Consider today's typical experience at a restaurant. You are likely to encounter a waiter or waitress who offers his or her first name before offering water. Something on the order of:

"Hi, I'm Jeffrey and I'll be your server today."

The practice is often at the direction of management, hoping, no doubt, to make diners feel welcome.

Or consider the setting of a hospital. No matter how many years of experience a nurse has or what her/his age, a nurse is likely to be referred to by first name while a doctor, even a fledging doc fresh out of medical school, is often conferred with a title and last name. Similarly, nurses often introduce themselves to patients with a first name only. According to authors Bernice Beresh and Suzanne Gordon, in *From Silence to Voice – What Nurses Know and Must Communicate to the Public,* "the subordination of nursing is constantly reintroduced and reinforced when doctors call nurses by their first name and nurses call doctors by their last name and title."[5]

Patients may also feel a lack of respect because of how they are addressed. One 2006 study encompassing several hundred European patients over the age of 65 found that many of the older participants disliked it when health or social care professionals called them pet names such as "dear" or "love" and thought it disrespectful when they were addressed by their first name without their consent.[6]

From "Yes, ma'am" to "Hey, babe"

The seminal studies governing forms of address were conducted in the 1960's. While the conclusions reached at that time on hierarchy and solidarity are still valid, it's also worthwhile to look at more recent studies and developments in our naming conventions.

One 1992 study examined the restaurant business, specifically at methods used to enforce the relatively low status accorded to waitresses. Both restaurant owners and male co-workers called female servers a number of slang and derogatory names such as "babe" or "wench." The authors concluded that such terms of address were used to reinforce the sexual division of labor as well as hierarchy.[7]

Gender often impacts the terms of address used. Despite the fact that women now increasingly hold comparable positions to men, they are not always accorded equal status by subordinates. A 2003 study examined how college students address their professors, noting whether they used first name only or a title and last name. Researchers found that male professors were much more likely to be referred to by their title than female professors.[8]

Titles can be important, particularly when someone feels, whether rightly or wrong, slighted by the omission of such. Recall the testy exchange between U.S. Senator Barbara Boxer and Brigadier General Michael Walsh at a 2009 Senate hearing. Walsh began his response to a question posed by Boxer with the term "Ma'am." Boxer interrupted.

"You know, do me a favor. Could you say senator instead of ma'am? ... It's just a thing. I worked so hard to get that title."[9]

Boxer evidently took the general's comment as a sign of disrespect, although she was probably wrong. Use of the term ma'am is customary in military courtesy when referring to a female officer.

Boxer is not the only woman to bristle at being referred to as "ma'am." This particular honorific (a shortened version of madame) was the subject of a New York Times writer's impromptu poll in 2010. Natalie Angier surveyed 27 professional women of varying occupations. Of that group, only two indicated they liked being called "ma'am," while 15 disliked it, some quite vehemently. Some said it made them feel old.[10]

What was once a word meant to convey courtesy and respect now, in some quarters, conveys a different meaning.

One of the internet survey respondents, a 55-year-old white female named Jane, described her reaction: "In the south, I am generally called ma'am, which causes me to feel rather old. During a trip to Puerto Rico, I was always referred to as Lady, which was somewhat charming."

First name familiarity and black holes

Informality is the watchword in many areas of our culture and forms of address are no exception.

Probably no incident better illustrates the dramatic change than Jon Stewart's 2010 interview with President Barack Obama. The President had just commented that a member of his administration had done a "heckuva job," a pointed reference to predecessor George W. Bush's assessment of FEMA official Michael Brown's handling of Hurricane Katrina relief efforts. Stewart blurted out: "You don't want to use that phrase, dude."

The slang term "dude," as one researcher puts it, references a demeanor of "cool solidarity" typically between men. More recently, women have begun to use the term, but they tend to do so, not as a greeting, but when commiserating with someone, issuing an order or confronting someone.[11]

Stewart's use of the term "dude," with its inference of informality and male chumminess, to refer to the President, had many cringing in horror. Obama later said he wasn't offended. Nonetheless, the very notion of such casualness in addressing a head of state would have been unthinkable in an earlier time. Similar, if less dramatic, signs of informality are everywhere.

One physician wrote in the New York Times about her constant discomfort when patients nowadays (most often men) call her by her first name. "It is almost always an older patient who will use my first name, in a friendly, offhand way," complained Dr. Anne Marie Valinoti. "Are they trying to be chummy? Is it a power thing, making them feel less vulnerable while they sit half naked on the exam table?" Her male colleagues, Valinoti added, have similar experiences. Despite that, she wrote, she rarely calls a patient by his or her first name, even teenagers.[12]

Shirley, a 55-year-old white physician who responded to the internet survey, wrote that she uses first name if the person was the same age, younger, a friend or colleague and *not* a patient. "Title + last name is preferred for older persons, casual acquaintances, clients/patients."

Author Ralph Keyes, however, contends that the increasing use of first names does not imply as much solidarity as one might think. First names, he wrote in a 2007 Christian Science Monitor article, can mean disrespect, particularly when coming from someone who does not know you. Keyes also notes a trend to abandon surnames and rely only on first names, even with strangers. "Far from being intimate, sharing first names alone is impersonal," he wrote. "Dispensing with surnames reflects wariness more than informality. In a guarded time like ours, revealing two names to another person ratchets up one's level of exposure."[13]

One of the more jarring facets of the television drama *Mad Men,* aside from the open and rampant sexism, is the rigid system whereby employees of the fictional Sterling Cooper ad agency address each other. In keeping with the mores of the '60's when the show takes place, the men are addressed as "Mr. Draper" or "Mr. Sterling," while the women (all of whom are subordinates when the show begins) are, without exception, called by their first names or else collectively as "girls."

In today's workplace not only are the overt displays of sexism recounted in Mad Men gone, but the rules by which we address each other have changed. Now informality is the norm.

Professor David Morand, who teaches management at Penn State, has written extensively about the linguistic changes that have taken place in today's business environment. Morand concluded that it is quite common for subordinates to call superiors – even CEO's – by their first name. In many companies, it has become standard corporate culture for all employees to interact on a first-name basis, with the aim of installing a company-wide sense of egalitarianism.[14]

For some employees, however, calling the company president (who is still your boss and holds the key to your job security) by his or her first name simply doesn't feel right. The quandary of those employees has produced what Morand calls a "black hole" of social space. Rather than use a first name, some employees go to great lengths and plan ways to avoid using *any* form of address at all.[15]

Several of the internet survey respondents were firm advocates for today's casual terms of address. One, a 16-year-old multi-racial male student identified as Shane, wrote: "I call everybody, even older people, by their first names if they are friends or acquaintances but I use Mr. or Mrs., when it is an older adult that is less of a friend but more of a friend's mother or something of the sort."

Tom, a 65-year-old white journalist, said he was "quite fond of first names and diminutives. ... I'm too egalitarian to like titles. If I can't call my doctor Jim, then I need to find another doctor." Yet, he added, casual could be problematic for a white man in addressing women and blacks. "Sometimes it is far better to use a title than to come off sounding patronizing or condescending."

Chapter Three
Tell Me Something Good

Try to think of all the people you know or encounter as you go through a typical day. Then take a look at the topics you discuss with them. If you are like many, you speak with some acquaintances about enjoyable pastimes, such as what music you enjoy or what film you saw over the weekend. With other friends, politics may be the favored subject. The conversation may be light and lively or loud and argumentative but the subjects up for discussion are not particularly personal.

With a few folks, however, you may broach other matters. You may vent about those bills that seem to be piling up or that meddling aunt who keeps showing up at your door and overstaying her welcome.

Your list may be smaller, however, when it comes to those people with whom you would share more intimate revelations such as worries about a recent medical test or fears about your sexual adequacy.

Now turn the tables. Consider what other people tell you about themselves. Who is it who routinely confides in you? Or does anyone?

You've just taken an informal measure of the self-disclosure in your relationships with others. Self-disclosure means revealing something about one's self to another person. Naturally, it is critical to developing and maintaining close relationships. We all know intuitively that the more intimate two people are, the more likely they are to share opinions, feelings, thoughts and desires.

Beyond that commonsense observation, however, let's examine how self-disclosure plays out in various situations and what it can tell us about the hierar-solidarity aspects of our relationships.

What, When, To Whom

Think back to when you were young and how your family may have gathered around the dinner table in the evening. What were the topics of conversation? In some households, subjects such as politics or religion may have been taboo, or "off the table," so to speak. The idea was that debate, and the inevitable disagreements that follow it, were to be avoided. (In fact, it was frequently considered rude or at the very least, overly nosy to ask someone how they cast their vote.) Other households, however, routinely had lively debates over their meal about the news of the day. Clearly, as cultural norms change, so do our views of what subject matter is appropriate to share with acquaintances and friends.

You may wonder what dinner-table conversations have to do with self-disclosure. Most of us think of "self-disclosure" as those deep, heartfelt conversations with our best friends or our lovers in which we confess our innermost hopes, dreams and fears. Certainly such confidences are self-disclosures of the most intimate kind.

But when psychologists talk about self-disclosure, they use the term in a much broader sense, one that includes the simple sharing of likes and dislikes, opinions and experiences. So when you tell your co-worker that you grew up in Biloxi and have two younger siblings, you're not exactly pouring out your heart. Nonetheless, you are offering up information about yourself. Or, when you tell your date that you hate vacationing in the mountains and much prefer the beach and you'd much rather read a paperback than an E-book any day, it's all self-disclosure. These revelations give the listener knowledge about what you think and how you approach life.

Two psychologists in 1958 devised a method to measure self-disclosure using a questionnaire with scored answers. The categories developed by Sidney Jourard and Paul Lasakow included:

• Attitudes and opinions about such matters as religion and social issues

• Tastes and interests, such as sports, fashion, food or books

• Work-related topics, including the pros and cons of one's job, feelings about co-workers, ambitions, etc.

The questionnaire also included the following more intimate/personal categories:

• Money matters, such as one's salary, debts, savings, worries, budget

• Personality-related topics, including things one is ashamed of or feels guilty about, things that make one angry and intimate relationship matters

• Body-related topics such as sexual enjoyment or difficulty, health concerns, like/dislike of one's own body, or weight problems.[1]

Given such a range of subject matter, disclosure can and does occur in a number of circumstances and between people interacting in various types of relationships. The conversation may be on a date, at a party, at work, on an airplane or at a bar. It may involve the best of friends, people of varying social status, or strangers.

Many of us have, on occasion, had to contend with the garrulous stranger on the next barstool who, unsolicited, proceeds to enumerate his many complaints about his girlfriend. Or you may have encountered the stressed woman in the grocery line, who loudly recounts last night's screaming match with her husband to no one in particular and in a voice designed for all to hear. These situations, however, are not the norm. In general, intimate revelations such as these are reserved for those with whom we are fairly close friends.

The internet survey provides a snapshot of the range of self-disclosure. Participants were given a list of five topic areas (social issues such as race and sexual orientation; work issues including ambitions or co-workers; money issues such as salary or debts; psychological issues including fears or self-esteem; appearance issues such as health or attractiveness), then asked if they discuss any of those subjects with others.

Mary, a 55-year-old white counselor, replied that "I am not very interested in conversations that do not contain self-disclosure, and I self-disclose a lot myself. I guess a lot of people are afraid of crossing certain boundaries but I think there is a big difference between getting into the other person's space and simply exchanging information on where I or the other person stands on the five issues."

But George, a multiracial man with a Bachelor's degree who is the same age as Mary, takes the opposite approach. "I generally avoid initiating or taking up discussion of any of the topics listed above in any but the closest social situations and with very specific individuals."

Others, however, indicated that they limit the subjects they are willing to discuss as well as with whom they speak. Tom, a 65-year-old white journalist, said he had always been comfortable speaking with African-Americans on matters of race. "But," he added, "until the last ten years I was too far in the closet to be able to discuss homosexuality, even in the vaguest of terms, with supposedly straight people." As for the other topics, Tom said if they came up, he spoke with "very carefully chosen words; no real conversation."

Obviously, individuals differ both in their ability and willingness to self-disclose. They also differ in how skilled they are at eliciting and encouraging disclosure from someone else. A person's cultural background can also affect how much he or she is willing to disclose.

With that said, how does self-disclosure relate to status and friendship? What clues can it offer us about how others regard us? We can make the following generalizations:

- The closer (greater friendship) two people are, the more likely they are to disclose something about themselves to each other

- People of the same social status are more likely to disclose to each other

•When the status (or perceived status) of two indi
viduals differs, the higher status person will be less
likely to disclose to the lower status person

Keep in mind that both status and friendship exist
on continuums. On one end of the friendship continuum,
you have those who are true intimates, while on the other,
you have those who are friends simply because they are of
a like mind or share various beliefs. That is, they may be-
long to the same club, work on the same political campaign, or subscribe to similar religious beliefs. Like-
minded people behave in a more relaxed manner with one
another and are therefore more likely to engage in self-
disclosure.

Disclosure, Trust and Likeability

Sharing personal information and confidences typically increases trust and likeability

The ability of self-disclosure to alter relationships
can be seen in various contexts, including the workplace.
Most of us have at some time had a boss who has issued a
standing invitation to bring any problems to his or her attention. "My door is always open," the saying goes. While
some supervisors are able to create a climate where employees are free to speak their mind, others are not. Those
who are successful at maintaining a true open-door policy
know a secret about self-disclosure: the best way to get
staff members to open up to you is to share a little bit

about yourself. That is, sharing some personal opinions with employees promotes greater trust. Even small talk about personal interests can improve supervisor/employee relations.

A word of caution: one 2003 study (appropriately entitled "Trust Me, I'm Your Boss") concluded that insincere efforts on the part of managers to ingratiate themselves via self-disclosure can be transparent and can produce greater distrust.[2]

As a general rule, self-disclosure is closely related to how much we like someone. Not only do we tend to confide more in people whom we like, we prefer those to whom we have already disclosed. What's more, people who disclose personal information are generally more liked than those who don't disclose.

That even goes for new acquaintances. Total strangers report increased feelings of social attraction toward their conversation partner when the get-acquainted talk includes such topics as personal interests, personality and future plans.[3] This is true for both men and women.[4]

Finally, you might be surprised to know that negative gossip, despite its potential for harm, can draw certain people together. A recent study found that when two people confide in each other their negative opinions of someone else, they feel closer to each other. Gossipers, it seems, can build a friendship when they share a dislike of someone else.[5]

You Tell Me and I'll Tell You

Everyone has had the experience of exchanging background information. We describe what part of the country we are from or where we attended school. One person begins and the other follows suit. The exchange of disclosures might proceed to tastes in music or movies and so on. What's going on here? One person's self-disclosure encourages the other (the listener) to recipro-cate, to share similar information.

The notion of reciprocity in self-disclosure can be seen in various contexts. Authority figures or those in a higher status position who want to encourage self-disclosure from subordinates often begin with admissions of their own. Supervisors are an obvious example, as dis-cussed previously. But the same holds true in other con-texts.

Lawyers seeking honest answers from jurors dur-ing the voir dire questioning process often reveal some-thing about themselves to jurors early in the process. A lawyer might say: "Since I've been the victim of a home burglary and been terribly upset by it, I would probably have a hard time being impartial if I were a juror on a bur-glary case." Such a statement tells the panel members a little about the lawyer's background and feelings. In turn, jurors are less reticent about discussing their own possi-ble preconceptions or biases.

The same holds true for other professionals. In the classroom, teacher self-disclosure can stimulate student class participation.[6] Doctors who share a bit of their backgrounds before conducting an examination can help patients feel both at ease and on a more equal footing. One physician's efforts to do so were documented in a 1996 study. In order to relate to her patients as equals, the doctor would discuss her own fears, interests and ideas. In one instance, she told a patient who was berating herself for failing to take a medication that she was "the same way. I mean I can see a lot of you in me and I've had to learn stuff."

Researchers who analyzed the doctor's dialogues with her patients concluded that "physician self-disclosure works to downplay perceived status differences and facilitate a cooperative, team approach to the health care encounter."[7]

In other words the doctor-patient relationship moved from a status relationship to one of equals who are friends.

Chapter Four
From Where I Sit

On Jan. 8, 2011, a disturbed 22-year-old man went on a shooting rampage at a supermarket parking lot in Tucson, Arizona. When it was over, six people were dead and 12 others, including the shooter's target -- U.S. Representative Gabrielle Giffords -- were wounded.

Many linked the tragedy to a high level of angry, extremist political rhetoric, citing such inflammatory incidents as the Sarah Palin campaign's placement of crosshairs on a map highlighting the districts of progressive Democrats, including that of Giffords.

In the weeks that followed, Congress took an unprecedented step. Evoking the need for civility in politics, a number of Senators and Representatives broke ranks and sat with a member of the opposing party for the occasion of the President's State of the Union address. The seat reshuffling was initiated by Senators Mark Udall of Colorado and Lisa Murkowski of Alaska. In a joint statement, eventually signed by numerous other members of the Senate and House, the two senators wrote that partisan seating on opposite sides of the House symbolized "division instead of the common challenges we face."[1] While not all in Congress embraced the bipartisan seating, others decided to try it out and sought out new seatmates for the evening.

The whole affair was obviously a symbolic and fleeting gesture of solidarity. But it also was a well-publicized illustration of the fact that where one sits in relation to someone else makes a statement, often a very political statement.

Consider the example of the Paris peace talks, convened in an attempt to negotiate an end to the war in Vietnam. The discussions hit a snag that lasted for months, all over the issue of seating arrangements. The North Vietnamese wanted the Viet Cong to be an equal party to the talks and so proposed a circular table, where all participants would be equals. The South Vietnamese, however, refused, arguing for a rectangular table to reinforce their position that only two sides were at issue in the negotiations. Eventually a compromise was reached. Representatives of the North and South Vietnamese governments were to sit at a circular table. Flanking the round table would be two square tables where representatives of the other parties would sit in close proximity to their allies.

Seating arrangements can also make a political statement on a much smaller, or "micropolitical," stage.

One's decision to sit – or not sit -- next to someone else may speak volumes about attitudes and politics. We've all seen people who are reluctant to sit with someone of a different race, ethnicity or sexual orientation and may even go out of their way to avoid doing so. One study took a look at the seating choices of homophobic people and found they were more likely to avoid sitting next to someone they believed homosexual if they could do so "covertly." In other words, if they could justify their decision on some other grounds.[2]

Seating, no doubt, sends a message, one that is sometimes loud and clear.

In the courtroom, the judge presides while seated behind a raised bench that may only be approached with permission. In the conference room, the chair of the day's meeting occupies a position at the head of the table in order to direct the discussion. The message in both scenarios? Power and status.

Very different, less formal arrangements convey a very different picture. In the restaurant, one might see two friends seated at the corners of the square table, chatting over appetizers. Or in the dimly lit nightclub, two lovers can be found snuggling side by side in a booth as they sip drinks. The message here is one of friendship and intimacy.

When it comes to seating, here are some basics:

• When we like someone, we choose to sit closer to them. So naturally when someone chooses to sit near us, we infer that they like us and thus tend to like them as well.

• We tend to sit further away from those who are of a higher or a lower status.

• People engage in more conversation when sitting in more immediate positions – meaning seats that are closer together or more directly oriented to each other.[3]

• Women prefer sitting side by side with friends more than men, who tend to prefer opposite seating.

When you consider the above points they probably correspond to your everyday experience. Tom, a journalist who was one of the internet survey responders, said when he is with a friend, they typically occupy the corners of a table. But if he is conducting an interview, he sits across the table – at a greater distance -- from the person he is interviewing. "I never really thought about why," he added.

Shane, a high school student who was also part of the internet survey, related similar experiences: "I sit face to face for dates or business/serious conversations and I sit side by side with friends."

Other survey respondents had somewhat different preferences. Joseph, a 35-year-old network consultant, said he has found "sitting face to face tends to encourage a more adversarial disposition, even between friends. Mary, a 55-year-old counselor, said she prefers to sit "across a corner, facing the other person. Side by side is ok, but then it's a bit uncomfortable to face the other person."

Conducive to conversation

Where you choose to sit in relation to someone you are speaking with obviously depends on what arrangements are available. Is there a table? Is it square, round or rectangular? Or is there a couch? Or a couch and two chairs grouping? Are the chairs movable?

Let's say you are meeting with a client in an office conference room at a typical rectangular-shaped table, as most tables in such settings are. You could sit at the head of the table and offer your client a seat at the opposite end. But the message is clear – this is not much of a cordial meeting. The two of you are pretty distant from one another in physical space, and may well be on the issues as well. This arrangement is not going to be conducive to a meeting of the minds.

Occupying face-to-face seats on the sides of the rectangular-shaped table would be a little friendlier arrangement, but still a bit adversarial. Sitting side by side on the same side of the table is friendlier still, but awkward for comfortable eye contact. That leaves the corner seats. If the two of you occupy the corners, two factors are at work: you are sitting closer, which typically sends a friendly message to your client, yet one of you has seat of distinction at the head of the table.

In fact, observers regard such a corner arrangement (in which one party is at the head of the table) to be significantly less equal than when two people are seated at both ends of the table or on both sides.[4]

Traditionally, the person at the head of the table acquires an aura of authority and status. At dinners, the family head would occupy that seat. At company meetings, senior management would sit there. In study after study, the person in a group who sits at the head of the table is regarded as the leader of the group. In one 1971 study, people were shown slides of five young women seated at a rectangular table, with one woman at the head and two others seated on each side. The observers, asked for their first impressions of all five women, rated the woman at head of the table higher on six different leadership qualities, including talkativeness, persuasiveness, dominance, self-confidence, intelligence and leadership.[5]

If the aim is to downplay status differences, square or round tables avoid the problem of having to decide who will occupy the seat at the head of the table. As the story goes, King Arthur chose a round table for convocations of his knights to promote equality and solidarity.

If you are leading a group discussion, however, and want to present yourself as more of an equal/friend, leave the head of the table seat open or for someone else and sit in the middle of the side. You'll get better eye contact with everyone and probably a better conversation.

Take a seat and the interview will begin

What about the typical workplace meeting between two people that occurs, not in a boardroom, but in an office? Suppose you're interviewing a recruit for a job opening that you badly need to fill. This particular person would be a perfect fit for the job and is someone you'd really like to hire. So you'd like her to feel welcome and comfortable. Take a look around your office. For starters, there's that giant desk. If you sit at your desk and she faces you, that desk is quite an imposing barrier.

Research tells us that women may be particularly influenced by the presence of that desk. One study interviewed women who had met a therapist for the first time and were asked to decide if they would like to hire him for future sessions. When the therapist was seated behind a desk for the interview, women gave the therapist lower ratings on attractiveness, expertise and trustworthiness. The same effect did not occur with men.[6]

So get out from behind the desk. Arrange some comfortable chairs together at right angles for good eye contact. You'll send a friendlier message. On the other hand, if you're speaking with a current employee to discuss his or her tardiness habit, you may want to convey authority and status. So sitting behind a desk may be the best choice in such a circumstance.

Seating arrangements definitely send a message to a person being interviewed, giving them a clue as to the atmosphere (friendly/unfriendly) they might expect to encounter at the company. What's more, seating can alter the course of the interview by affecting how well an applicant performs.

We already know that seating can impact the amount of conversation. In an interview situation, researchers found that seating distances can affect the demeanor and performance of an applicant, and, that white interviewers choose to sit further away from black applicants than from white applicants.

Here's how the two related experiments, published in 1974, were carried out:

White male college students who had been told they would be interviewing applicants for a marketing campaign came into the interview room to meet the "applicants," who were black and white high school students. The "interviewers" promptly discovered that the room had no chair for them to sit in while conducting the interview, so they had to get a chair from the room next door. This deliberate omission meant that the interviewer would have to choose where to place the chair in relation to the applicant. The interviewers – all of whom were white – placed their chairs closer to white applicants (an average of 58 inches away) and further away from black applicants (an average of 62 inches away). Researchers concluded that the four-inch difference between the two average distances was a statistically significant amount.

In the second experiment, white male college students were asked to serve as applicants and help train job interviewers. The interviewers in this instance were members of the research team who intentionally sat either close to the applicant in a chair at the side of the table, or far away from the applicant, in a chair behind the table and opposite the applicant. The distances used by the interviewers were similar to the average distances from the first experiment, but were maximized by the added factor of having the interviewer sit either behind or at the side of the table. Two judges who were not part of the research team evaluated the interviews and rated the applicants. Applicants in the "far" seating arrangement were found inadequate more often, as well as nervous.

Researchers concluded that differing treatment of black and white applicants, such as occurred with seating arrangements in the first experiment, can and does affect the attitudes and performance of job candidates. These findings provide a cautionary note that the setting of an interview, particularly when individuals of different races are involved, can negatively impact how well an applicant does.[7]

Chapter Five

Here's Lookin' At You

To be successful, every aspiring politician must master the basics of "working" a room full of voters. Specifically, he or she must learn to smile, to grasp the voter's hand firmly (but not too hard), and to look him or her straight in the eye when speaking. The most adept politicians, however, can transfer that one-to-one skill to much bigger venues, including to a television audience of millions. John Kennedy demonstrated such expertise during the 1960 presidential debate, which, by all accounts, he won handily. One of the keys to his triumph was eye contact: Kennedy looked directly into the camera with each answer, almost as though he were having a conversation directly with each voter. Richard Nixon, on the other hand, would at times look to his side, toward the panel of journalists and away from the camera, during his answers.

In politics as well as in our everyday encounters, the direct look inspires confidence and trust.

People comply with a request more often, donate more money, and are more likely to take a leaflet when the person making the request makes direct eye contact. What's more, the longer the solicitor or interviewer looks someone in the eye, the more favorably that solicitor/ interviewer is judged.[1] Passersby are much more likely (66% versus 34%) to agree to take a survey if the solicitor maintains eye contact than if the solicitor looks away as soon as others look at him/her.[2]

Nonverbal signals can let others know you are available and willing to engage in conversation. Specifically, making eye contact can send a message of friendliness and encourage others to approach you, whether you are a salesperson in the department store or a reference librarian. In fact, eye contact was the reason most frequently mentioned by library users in one study for choosing to approach a particular librarian for assistance.[3] On the other hand, looking away from someone you encounter or evading their glance sends the opposite message: conversation is probably not welcome right now.

Looking at lovers and superiors

Most of us naturally tend to look more often at our friends than at strangers we encounter. But, lovers have a special way about them when it comes to eye contact. Simply put, they like to gaze at each other. Romantic partners look at each other for longer periods of time than they look at their friends.[4]

Lovers may get the longest gazes, but we also tend to make more eye contact with those people we believe to be important or of a higher status than ourselves. Conversely, we look less at those we believe to be of lower status or less important than ourselves. That's why the male car salesman attempting to convince a couple to buy the latest model, may direct his pitch – and much of his eye contact – to the husband whom he believes to be "in charge" of such matters (of greater importance when it comes to the decision to purchase). He may, however, be wrong on that score and might be better advised to divide his eye contact between both husband and wife.

Visual attentiveness to higher status individuals is likely to be greater in situations where hierarchical differences are institutionally defined (i.e., law enforcement or the military). In one study, researchers monitored conversations between 20 pairs of student ROTC members. Each pair had one officer and one cadet, thereby invoking a clear hierarchy. In addition, the officer in each pair was allowed to determine how much of a reward the cadet would receive at the end of each exercise. Time and again, the lower-ranking cadets were visually more attentive to the officers during conversation than the officers were to the lower ranking cadets.

A second and related experiment compared the amount of eye contact between two different groups of people in pairs. One was a group that paired ROTC officers with cadets. Here, the status distinction was obvious. The other group paired one student with another, both from a gym class. In order to create an artificial status distinction between the gym students, one student was given the power to determine the reward his or her partner would receive at the end of the exercise.

In both situations, the lower status person made more eye contact during conversation.

Researchers then compared the two groups. Overall, the ROTC cadets, with their formalized and rigid hierarchy, were more attentive to their conversation partner than the lower-status gym students to their partner.[5]

Is timing everything?

While the duration of eye contact is important, there is a more critical characteristic of how we look at our conversation partners that is even more revealing about hierarchy and solidarity. That characteristic is *when* we make eye contact and *when* we don't. Are we looking while we are speaking? Looking while we are listening? Or at both times?

You may recall a time when, as a child, you got a stern lecture from a parent. You may have squirmed uncomfortably and looked down at the floor, all the while wishing you were somewhere -- anywhere -- else. Odds are you heard this admonition from mom or dad: "Look at me when I'm talking to you!" That's because looking at your conversation partner (even a parental one) while he or she is speaking signals respect and, in some instances, submission.

The rule of thumb is this: a higher status/power person will look at the other person more while speaking than while listening. The lower status/power person looks more while listening than while speaking.

Take for instance, the officer/cadet ROTC conversationalists. The cadets looked at the officers much more when listening than when speaking.[6]

So, when the chair of your meeting or your boss looks at you while speaking, that is to be expected, since he/she is in a position of authority at the time. But where is the chair/boss looking while others—including you -- are speaking? Looking down at one's notes, at the clock or out the window while someone else is speaking sends a pretty clear message: you and what you are saying just isn't important.

Social scientists have established a measure to quantify the manner in which eye contact and status/power are linked. The Visual Dominance Ratio (VDR) is the relationship between the time spent looking at a conversation partner when speaking and the time spent looking at that person while listening. High power/status individuals look at the other person more when speaking than when listening. When the two people engaged in a conversation differ in power or status, the lower status person looks at their conversation partner more when listening than when speaking.

Gender and race can impact both when and how much eye contact is made.

When the two parties to a conversation are a man and woman, matters get a little more complicated. When the higher status of one or the other is quite clear, that person – whether man or woman – looks more while speaking than while listening and the other looks more while listening. But when the two are of equal status, the man tends to make eye contact (more while speaking than listening) as if he were in the position of power, even when he is not.[7]

Some older studies indicate that blacks who are listeners in a conversation tend to make less eye contact than whites. They look away from the speaker more often than whites in the same position do.[8] Furthermore, black students in a conversation with their teacher were found to make minimal eye contact while listening. When the teacher is white, he or she may interpret the lack of eye contact as a lack of respect or attention to the topic at hand.[9]

The look of power

Eye contact can express our attitudes (solidarity/ hierarchy) toward others. At the same time, we make assumptions about others' attitudes toward us based on clues such as eye contact. That means we tend to judge people who look more while talking (who have a high visual dominance ratio or VDR) to be more powerful or of a higher status, and those who look more while listening to be less powerful.[10]

In the ROTC example discussed earlier, researchers discovered that the officers who looked more at cadets during conversations were the same officers who received lower ratings in leadership.[11] In a study conducted in Japan, patients (who were actors with a given scenario) were interviewed by medical students. The "patients" then rated the medical students' interviews. The ratings were higher when the students looked at them equally while speaking and listening.[12]

A recent study found that we are pretty good at judging someone's socioeconomic status based on his or her nonverbal behaviors while listening, including eye contact. Individuals of higher status, the researchers found, signal their status by disengaging, including fidgeting, doodling and failing to make eye contact with the speaker. Low status individuals, on the other hand, were attentive to speakers and kept eye contact while listening. When observers watched videos of conversations, they were successful at guessing the person's socioeconomic status with better than chance accuracy.[13]

Chapter Six

The Magic Touch

In 2011, The Miami Heat, with their newly-acquired star Lebron James, were heavy favorites to win the NBA championship, yet lost in the finals to the Dallas Mavericks. Not everyone however was shocked. After Game 4, with the series tied 2-2, one team of newspaper analysts (from the Wall Street Journal of all places!) speculated that Dallas just might have the right formula to win. According to the WSJ, the Mavs seemed to have the magic touch – quite literally. That is, they touched their teammates with high fives, butt slaps, chest pats or hugs way more than Heat players did.

WSJ staffers had scrutinized broadcasts of the first three games, ignoring the usual field goal, assist and foul stats. Instead they logged every time teammates could be seen touching each other. The data was compiled in a chart called "The Touchy-Feely Index." Simply put, it showed Dallas players touched teammates nearly twice as much as their opponents.[1]

To give credit where credit is due, the inspiration for the WSJ analysis was a well-publicized research study by three Berkeley professors with the decidedly unglamorous name, "Tactile Communication, Cooperation and Performance: An Ethological Study of the NBA." These scholarly researchers had logged the teammate touches of 294 NBA players drawn from all 30 teams. Their conclusion: teams whose players touched each other more often, won more often.[2]

If chest bumps can boost a team to a championship, what can less dramatic, more commonplace touches do? Well, even a light touch can be a powerful and persuasive tool. It can increase one's likelihood of success in getting another to comply with a request, such as filling out a survey or signing a petition. It can even increase tips.

Sound far-fetched? Consider this 2003 study, in which researchers kept track of the tips given by 400 diners to four servers in two different restaurants. The data showed that when the waiter or waitress briefly and lightly touched the customer on the shoulder when returning change, the result was a bigger tip.[3]

When it comes to getting people to go along with a request, a light touch works wonders. It even helps in courtship. French researchers tried using light touches on the forearm to see if that would increase the odds of young men's success in getting women to dance to a slow song in a nightclub or just getting phone numbers from women they approached on the street. In both instances, a one to two second touch on the arm, got better results for the amorous young men. The success rate for attempts to collect phone numbers on the street nearly doubled (from 10% to 19.2%) when the request was accompanied by a brief touch.[4]

On a less romantic but no less remarkable note, another French experiment showed that when touched lightly, people are more agreeable to helping out a stranger, even one who asks a rather big favor. In this instance, passersby on a busy street were asked to watch a large, rather excited dog while the owner went into a nearby pharmacy for 10 minutes. Those who received a simple touch were more amenable to hanging onto the dog's leash.[5]

The message of touch

Even the briefest touch somehow seems to communicate volumes. It connects us with others. Critical to understanding exactly what message a given touch conveys is the type, duration and frequency of touching involved. In the context of a conversation, touches might include handshakes, hugs, handholding, a pat on the shoulder, or a simple light touch to the forearm.

A touch can convey trust, credibility, empathy, good will and, of course, affection. It can also, however, signal dominance, status and power. In one well known study, a researcher spent 60 hours observing and cataloguing the interactions of people in public places in the Boston area, noting if they touched at all, who touched whom and whether the touch was reciprocated. The observer also recorded their age, sex, and race and approximated their socio-economic status. The significant finding? *Higher status people touched lower status people more frequently*. The author of the study, noted psychologist Nancy Henley, concluded that touch might be called a "privilege" of status. Nonetheless, she added, it can also express solidarity.

"The hypothesis that touch communicates status is not necessarily in conflict with an alternative interpretation, that it communicates closeness," Henley wrote. "[U]sed reciprocally it indicates solidarity; when nonreciprocal, it indicates status."[6] In other words, when just one party to a conversation or interaction does the touching, the message is one of dominance and status, but when both parties touch each other, the message is friendlier.

Henley's conclusion that higher status people have a "privilege" to touch, a prerogative not shared by those of lower authority or status, seems to apply, even in instances where status is a temporary condition. In one experiment, students were paired and randomly assigned to act as teacher or student. Having assumed that role, the "teacher" proceeded to talk and interrupt more than the student did. The teacher also touched the student and his or her possessions more than the student touched the teacher. Here, status – even fleeting and arbitrarily-designated status – controlled the participant's nonverbal behavior.[7]

Status also impacts the type of touch used in various situations. One example is the manner in which people greet one another. Those with greater authority or power tend to initiate conversation by either a touch to the arm or a pat on the shoulder. Subordinates, on the other hand, approach others with a handshake.[8]

As we all know, a single touch can convey the closest intimacy. When lovers hold hands or touch each other's face, the message is clear. But even brief touches during a conversation can boost the credibility as well as the attractiveness of the person doing the touching.[9]

The number of touches made is also an indicator as to the intimacy of the relationship. Not surprisingly, people touch their romantic partners during conversation more frequently than do friends or acquaintances. Researchers were able to document this by cataloguing dozens of videotaped interactions. On an average, people touched their romantic partners three times during a six minute conversation. In contrast, male friends never touched during the same timeframe.[10]

One thing to keep in mind: context can be critical. Touches, even though they might be meant as friendly gestures, don't always have a positive impact. In the wrong situation, even an innocuous pat on the shoulder can have negative consequences. Another recent study bears that out.

In that Belgium experiment, participants competed against a partner (who was a confederate of the researchers) in a maze race. The race was rigged so the participant always won. But before the pair left the room to move onto the next game, the confederate patted the participant three times on the shoulder, smiled and wished them good luck. The next game involved participants choosing how many rewards to share with their partners (the confederates). A control group went through the exact same process except that no participants were patted on the shoulder.

When the data was tallied, it showed that participants who received pats on the shoulder shared fewer rewards with their partner. The friendliness offered by the confederate's physical gesture evidently produced a completely opposite effect. This held true even when participants didn't remember being patted on the shoulder.

It's unclear whether the pat on the shoulder was interpreted as condescension or as a sign of dominance. But, unlike the NBA teammates whose touches sparked cooperation, this touch, made in a competitive situation, had the opposite effect.[11]

Chapter Seven
The "You"
In Your Conversation Style

In the course of every conversation, be it long or short, significant or trivial, we convey something important about ourselves. Like it or not, we send signals about the nature of our attitudes and feelings toward the other person. Some clues are verbal – the words we choose and the subject matter we discuss. Others are non-verbal – the seat we choose and how often we make eye contact or touch.

If you are a careful conversationalist, you can learn to read these clues. You can discover if others regard you as a friend and equal or as only an acquaintance of unequal status. You can also become aware of how *you* are perceived. What attitudes about friendship or status do *you* project when speaking to others?

Let's review what we know so far.

The primary clues of conversation are these: address, self-disclosure, seating, eye contact and touch. If the speakers are:

GOOD FRIENDS OF EQUAL STATUS

Then:

Address → First Name/Nickname

Self-disclosure → Reveal private information

Seating → Side-by-Side/sit at corner

Eye-Contact → Similar speaking & listening

Touch → Frequent

ACQUAINTANCES OF UNEQUAL STATUS

Then:

Address → Title/Title+Last Name

Self-disclosure → Do not reveal private information

Seating → Face-to-Face/Head of table

Eye-Contact → High status: more while speaking

→ Low status: more while listening

Touch → Infrequent/Never

Status should not determine conversation style. The fact that you may be a supervisor and consequently hold higher office than your co-workers doesn't mean you must speak to them with an attitude or air of status. You may be a boss, but your conversational style can be one of solidarity and friendship.

A word of caution: The five conversational clues discussed in this book should not be taken as a sure-fire way to "read" another person, but rather as a tool to understand how you appear to others and how to improve your relationships with them.

The good news, however, is that these five signs are both easy to observe and easy to change. Every day, you will find new occasions to watch how conversations unfold as well as to improve your own speaking and listening style.

Endnotes:

Chapter Two:

Terms of Endearment, Terms of Estrangement

[1] Roger Brown and Albert Gilman, "The Pronouns of Power and Solidarity," in Thomas A. Sebeok (ed.) *Style in Language* (Cambridge: MIT Press, 1960), pp. 253-276.

[2] Roger Brown and Marguerite Ford, "Address in American English," *Journal of Abnormal & Social Psychology* (1961), Vol. 62, pp. 375-385.

[3] Dan I. Slobin, Stephen H. Miller and Lyman W. Porter, "Forms of address and social relations in a business organ-

ization," *Journal of Personality and Social Psychology,* (1968), Vol. 8(3), pp. 289-293.

[4] R.L. McNeely and Mary Kenny Badami, "Interracial communication in school social work," *Social Work,* (1984), Vol. 29(1), p. 22-25.

[5] Bernice Beresh and Suzanne Gordon, *From Silence to Voice – What Nurses Know and Must Communicate to the Public* (Ithaca, NY: Cornell University Press, 2006), p. 45.

[6] Gillian Woolhead , Win Tadd, Josep Antoni Boix-Ferrer, Stefan Krajcik, Barbara Schmid-Pfahler, Barbro Spjuth, David Stratton and Paul Dieppe, " 'Tu' or 'Vous?' A European qualitative study of dignity and communication with older people in health and social care settings," *Patient Education and Counseling* (2006), Vol. 61, pp. 363-371.

[7] Eleanor LaPointe, "Relationships with waitresses: gendered social distance in restaurant hierarchies," *Qualitative Sociology,* (1992), Vol. 15(4), 377-394.

[8] Hilary A. Takiff, Diana T. Sanchez and Tracie L. Stewart, "What's in a name? The status implications of students' terms of address for male and female professors," *Journal of Personality and Social Psychology,* (2001), Vol. 25(2), p. 134-144.

[9] The quotation is taken from an abridged hearing transcript found in "Please Don't Call Me Ma'am," National Public Radio *Talk of the Nation*, Sept. 8, 2010. The video exchange between the Senator and the General can be found on youtube.com.

[10] Natalie Angier, "The Politics of Polite," *New York Times*, August 28, 2010.

[11] Scott F. Kiesling, "Dude," *American Speech*, (2004), Vol. 79(3), p. 281-305.

[12] Anne Marie Valinoti, "Exam Room Rules: What's in a Name?" *New York Times*, December 14, 2009.

[13] Ralph Keyes, "What We Give Up by Using First Names," *Christian Science Monitor*, September 21, 2007, p. 9.

[14] David A. Morand, "Forms of Address and Status Leveling in Organizations," *Business Horizons*, November-December 1995, p. 34-39.

[15] David A. Morand, "Black Holes in Social Space: The Occurrence and Effects of Name-Avoidance in Organiza-

tions," *Journal of Applied Social Psychology*, (2005) Vol. 35 (2), pp. 320-334.

Chapter Three:

Tell Me Something Good

[1] Sidney M. Jourard and Paul Lasakow, "Some Factors in Self-Disclosure," *Journal of Abnormal and Social Psychology*, 1958, Vol. 56(1), pp. 91-98.

[2] Michael Willemyns, Cynthia Gallois and Victor J. Callan, "Trust Me, I'm Your Boss: Trust and Power in Supervisor-Supervisee Communication," *International Journal of Human Resource Management*, 2003, Vol. 14(1), pp. 117-127.

[3] Jeffrey R. Vittengl and Craig S. Holt, "Getting Acquainted: The Relationship of Self-Disclosure and Social Attraction to Positive Affect," *Journal of Social and Personal Relationships*, 2000, Vol. 17(1), pp. 53-66.

[4] Ruth Anne Clark, Michael Dockum, Heidi Hazeu, Meikuan Huang, Nan Luo, Jason Ramsey and Angel Spyrou, "Initial Encounters of Young Men and Women: Impressions and Disclosure Estimates," *Sex Roles*, 2004, Vol. 50(9/10), pp. 699-709.

[5] Jonathan R. Weaver and Jennifer K. Bosson, "I Feel Like I Know You: Sharing Negative Attitudes of Others Promotes Feelings of Familiarity," *Personality and Social Psychology Bulletin,* Vol. 37(4), pp. 481-491.

[6] Gary S. Goldstein and Victor A. Benassi, "The Relation Between Teacher Self-Disclosure and Student Classroom Participation," *Teaching of Psychology,* 1994, Vol. 21(4), pp. 212-217.

[7] Athena A. Smith-Dupre and Christina S. Beck, "Enabling Patients and Physicians to Pursue Multiple Goals in Health Care Encounters," *Health Communication,* 1996, Vol. 8(1), pp. 73-90.

Chapter Four:

From Where I Sit

[1] Mark Udall, Letter to Congressional Leadership Regarding Bipartisan Seating at the State of the Union Address, January 19, 2011. From markudall.senate.gov /? p=press_release&id=879.

[2] Melanie A. Morrison and Todd G. Morrison, "Development and Validation of a Scale Measuring Modern

Prejudice toward Gay Men and Lesbian Women," *Journal of Homosexuality,* 2002, Vol. 43(2), pp. 15-37.

[3] Albert Mehrabian and Shirley G. Diamond, "Seating Arrangement and Conversation," *Sociometry,* (1971) Vol. 34 (2), pp. 281-289.

[4] Nancy Felipe Russo, "Connotations of Seating Arrangements," *Cornell Journal of Social Relations,* 1967, Vol. 2, pp. 37-44.

[5] Robert J. Pelligrini, "Some Effects of Seating Position on Social Perception," *Psychological Reports,* 1971, Vol. 28, pp. 887-893.

[6] Carlton S. Gass, "Therapeutic Influence as a Function of Therapist Attire and the Seating Arrangement in an Initial Interview," *Journal of Clinical Psychology,* 1984, Vol. 40(1), pp. 52-57.

[7] Carl O. Word, Mark P. Zanna and Joel Cooper, "The Nonverbal Mediation of Self-Fulfilling Prophecies in Interracial Interaction," 1974, *Journal of Experimental Social Psychology,* Vol. 10, pp. 109-120.

Chapter Five:

Here's Lookin' At You

[1] Charles I. Brooks, Michael A. Church and Lance Fraser, "Effects of Duration of Eye Contact on Judgments of Personality Characteristics," *The Journal of Social Psychology,* 1986, Vol. 126(1), pp. 71-78.

[2] Nicolas Guéguen and Céline Jacob, "Direct Look Versus Evasive Glance and Compliance with a Request," *The Journal of Social Psychology,* 2002, Vol. 142(3), pp. 393-396.

[3] Marie L. Radford, "Approach or Avoidance? The Role of Nonverbal Communication in the Academic Library User's Decision to Initiate a Reference Encounter," *Library Trends,* 1998, Vol. 46(4), 699-718.

[4] Laura K. Guerrero, "Nonverbal Involvement Across Interactions with Same-Sex Friends, Opposite-Sex Friends and Romantic Partners: Consistency or Change?" *Journal of Social and Personal Relationships,* 1997, Vol. 14(1), pp. 31-58.

[5] Ralph V. Exline, Steve L. Ellyson and Barbara Long, "Visual Behavior as an Aspect of Power Role Relation-

ships," Chapter 2 of *Nonverbal Communication of Aggression*, 1975, New York: Plenum Press, pp. 21-52.

[6] Ibid.

[7] John F. Dovidio, Steve L. Ellyson, Caroline F. Keating, Karen Heltman and Clifford E. Brown, "The Relationship of Social Power to Visual Displays of Dominance Between Men and Women," *Journal of Personality & Social Psychology*, 1988, Vol. 54(2), pp. 233-242.

[8] Marianne LaFrance and Clara Mayo, "Racial Differences in Gaze Behavior During Conversations: Two Systematic Observational Studies," *Journal of Personality and Social Psychology*, 1976, Vol. 33(5), pp. 547-552.

[9] McNeely, op. cit.

[10] John F. Dovidio and Steve L. Ellyson, "Decoding Visual Dominance: Attributions of Power Based on Relative Percentages of Looking While Speaking and Looking While Listening," *Social Psychology Quarterly*, 1982, Vol. 45(2), pp. 106-113.

[11] Exline, op. cit.

[12] Hirono Ishikawa, Hideki Hashimoto, Makoto Kinoshita, Shin Fujimori, Teruo Shimizu and Eiji Yano, "Evaluating Medical Students' Non-Verbal Communication During the Objective Structured Clinical Examination," *Medical Education,* 2006, Vol. 40, pp. 1180-1187.

[13] Michael W. Kraus and Dacher Keltner, "Signs of Socioeconomic Status: A Thin-Slicing Approach," *Psychological Science,* 2009, Vol. 20(1), pp. 99-106.

Chapter Six:

The Magic Touch

[1] Scott Cacciola, "Dallas's Secret Weapon: High Fives," *Wall Street Journal,* June 9, 2011.

[2] Michael W. Kraus, Cassy Huang and Dacher Keltner, "Tactile Communication, Cooperation, and Performance: An Ethological Study of the NBA," *Emotion,* Vol. 10(5), pp. 745-749.

[3] Amy S. Ebesu Hubbard, A. Alen Tsuji, Christine Williams and Virgilio Seatriz Jr., "Effects of Touch on Gratuities Re-

ceived in Same-Gender and Cross-Gender Dyads," *Journal of Applied Social Psychology,* 2003, Vol. 33(11), pp. 2427-2438.

[4] Nicolas Guéguen, "Courtship Compliance: The Effect of Touch on Women's Behavior," *Social Influence,* 2007, Vol. 2 (2), pp. 81-97.

[5] Nicolas Guéguen and Jacques Fischer-Lokou, "An Evaluation of Touch on a Large Request: A Field Setting," *Psychological Reports,* 2002, Vol. 90, pp. 267-269.

[6] Nancy M. Henley, "Status and Sex: Some Touching Observations," *Bulletin of the Psychonomic Society,* 1973, Vol. 2 (2), pp. 91-93.

[7] Ann Leffler, Dair L. Gillespie and Joseph C. Conaty, "The Effects of Status Differentiation on Nonverbal Behavior," *Social Psychology Quarterly,* 1982, Vol. 45(3), pp. 153-161.

[8] Judith A. Hall, "Touch, Status and Gender at Professional Meetings," *Journal of Nonverbal Behavior,* 1996, Vol. 20(1), pp. 23-44.

[9] Judee K. Burgoon, Joseph B. Walther and E. James Baesler, "Interpretations, Evaluations, and Consequences of Interpersonal Touch," *Human Communication Research,* 1992, Vol. 19(2), pp. 237-263.

[10] Guerrero, op.cit.

[11] Jeroen Camps, Chloe Tuteleers, Jeroen Stouten and Jill Nelissen, "A Situational Touch: How Touch Affects People's Decision Behavior," *Social Influence,* 2012, iFirst, pp. 1-14.

Other books by Norman Markel

Psycholinguistics (1969)

Semiotic Psychology (1998)

The Five Vital Signs of Conversation (2009)

The Politics of Conversation (2013)